Wild Animal Families

by MARGARET DAVIDSON

illustrated by FRAN STILES

SCHOLASTIC INC.

New York Toronto London Auckland Sydney

Especially for Beatrice de Regniers—
a wonderful editor, a wonderful friend.

ISBN 0-590-45532-X

12 11 10 9 8 7 6 5 4 3 2 1   3   2 3 4 5 6 7/9

Printed in the U.S.A.   23

CONTENTS

Introduction

Right this minute — high in the mountains, deep in the ground, and under the water too — animals are being born.

A sea turtle lays a hundred eggs in a sandy nest...and crawls away. A frog leaves thousands of eggs in the mud by the side of some pond...and hops off. An oyster opens its shell and millions of eggs float out. Then its job is done.

When these eggs hatch, not one of the baby animals will ever be fed, or cared for, or taught a single thing. From the very beginning they will be left to live or die alone.

But for others the beginning of life is very different.

This book is about a group of animals called mammals. The smallest mouse is a mammal. And so is the biggest elephant. Humans are mammals too. What could these very different animals have in common?

Almost all mammals have some hair or fur on their bodies. All mammals are warm-blooded. This means the temperature of their bodies stays the same — no matter where they happen to be. All mammal mothers feed their babies milk when they are first born. And all mammal mothers care for their babies during the most dangerous time the young animals will ever know — the first days of life.

A baby is born

Before any animal can be born it must grow. Most mammals grow first inside their mothers' bodies, kept safe inside a kind of hollow place called the womb.

For some, this growing time is short. Hamster babies grow inside their mother's body for only 15 days, and then they are born. Wolf cubs take nine weeks.

For others, the time is longer. A human child grows in its mother's womb for nine months. A whale stays inside its mother for a year. It takes 22 months — almost two years — before an elephant baby is ready to be born.

But finally, for all, the moment comes. The first day of life!

When you were born your mother probably had help. Very likely you were born in a hospital with doctors and nurses nearby. But most wild animal mothers give birth alone.

A female deer goes deep into the forest. There, in some secret place, her two little fawns will be born.

When a female wolf is about to give birth, she goes into a safe dark den by herself. After her cubs are born she won't let any other wolf near them until they are a few weeks old. Not even her mate.

A wolf mother knows it is safer to keep the other wolves away at this time. Other members of the wolf pack she lives with are big and strong. Sometimes they play rough games. So they might hurt the new babies by mistake.

Other animals might hurt a baby on purpose. A grown male bear will eat almost anything. A few of his favorite foods are fish, mice, berries, gobs of honey — and tasty baby bears.

But not all mothers are quite so alone. A mother dolphin gets help for many months from another female dolphin called an *auntie*. The mother swims on one side of her baby. The auntie swims on the other side. There is no way a hungry killer whale or shark can turn *this* little dolphin into its next meal.

Every minute or so a baby dolphin must rise to the top of the water for a quick breath of air. Most of the time the baby can do this by itself. But sometimes it gets tired. It doesn't seem to know which way is up. Even now the little dolphin is in no danger. The mother and auntie are right there, waiting to push it the right way.

Some land babies have aunties too. A number of different giraffe mothers may leave their babies with another female giraffe. Sometimes this giraffe baby-sitter finds she is taking care of six or seven small giraffes at the same time. The job isn't too hard. This long-necked animal is so tall she can see most dangers when they are still far away. Elephant mothers also have help. So do lions and coyotes and some monkeys.

Mealtime

All mammal mothers feed their babies just one thing at first — milk.

Once some scientists found a baby walrus on a lonely beach. Its mother must have died. The men knew it couldn't live much longer without the right kind of food. But what could they feed the little walrus in place of its mother's rich milk?

The men poured heavy cream into a bowl. They mixed in cod-liver oil, a handful of vitamins, and some brewer's yeast. They added melted margarine and dropped in a few bits of chopped herring. Then they whirled the thick mixture in a blender.

Did the baby walrus like this smelly stuff? It drank its first bottle without stopping. Then it begged for more!

You probably drank your own mother's milk when you were a baby — or the milk of a cow. But if someone gave you the milk of a walrus, you would have been very sick. Walrus milk is *far* too rich for a human baby.

When you were a baby you probably ate any time you felt like it — day or night. But many animals must wait days or even weeks between meals.

A fur seal stays with her baby for about eight days. Then she goes to sea to feed herself. If she has to swim far to find food, she may not come back to nurse her child again for a whole week. A human baby would surely starve if it had to wait this long!

Many babies can take as long as they want to eat.

But others must take their meals in a gulp. Mammal babies that nurse underwater can't stay there for long. They would drown.

A mother whale or dolphin has special muscles in each of her two breasts. When her baby wants to nurse, the mother tightens these muscles and squirts a big helping of milk into her baby's mouth.

A newborn blue whale is the biggest baby in the world. It is as long as 15 human babies all in a line and weighs more than 500 babies! When it nurses, it swallows about 125 liters of milk at a time. That's a whole bathtub full of milk. No wonder the blue whale baby gains about five kilos* an hour!

*About 11 pounds

First homes

Baby dolphins spend all their time swimming through the water. A newborn elephant wanders with the rest of the herd right away. But many other animal babies stay in one place at first.

A mother rabbit usually digs a nest in the ground for her newborn babies. It is not much bigger than a soup bowl. How can a nest like this keep any animal safe?

The mother rabbit hides her children under a special blanket — a blanket she makes out of long blades of grass and her own soft rabbit fur. You could walk right by the little rabbits and not see them at all.

Raccoon babies live with their mother in a hollowed-out hole halfway up the trunk of a tree.

Wolf cubs cuddle close together in a dark den or cave. At first their mother never leaves them at all. The other grown-up members of the pack bring her food. Finally, after many weeks, she leads her little ones outside for the first time.

Polar bears are born in midwinter in the icy Far North — a time of howling winds and swirling snow and bitter cold. They are very tiny. Each little bear is about as big as two snowballs. And they are almost without fur. But their mother keeps them toasty warm — in the middle of a snow bank.

Long before they are born, the mother-to-be scoops out a deep hole in the snow. Then she settles down for a long winter's sleep.

Slowly more and more snow drifts over her body. Soon she is buried deep in it. Outside it is far below freezing. But the heat of her body keeps warming the air in her cave of snow.

Then one day her two cubs are born. The sleepy bear licks them dry. She does this to keep them clean. Licking is also a polar bear's way of petting her children—her way of saying "I love you." When the little cubs are clean and dry, the mother bear curls her body around them and settles down for another long nap.

It's very dark down in the snowy cave. But every time she wakes up she knows her babies are well. She can feel them snuggling close to her body. And she can hear them too. When bear cubs are happy they purr. They sound just like a litter of kittens—only louder.

Many animals are born underground. A mother prairie dog spends days digging her home. Often her mate helps her. When she is finished, a long tunnel

runs deep under the ground. Many shorter tunnels lead off this main one.

Each tunnel room is used for only one thing. One is the mother's bedroom. Another is the nursery where her babies will stay. Tasty plants and grasses and weeds and seeds are stored in the tunnel that serves as a kitchen. The prairie dog even digs a special tunnel for the family bathroom.

Keeping the babies safe

Some animals can take care of themselves when they are very young. Whales and other water babies can see and hear as soon as they are born. And, of course, they can swim.

Many land animals take their first steps soon after they are born. A zebra is born with long, strong legs. It can walk when it's only a few minutes old. A gazelle can run beside its mother in just one hour.

But some animal babies are quite helpless. They can't see or hear a thing. Some can't swim or walk or run. So they must be protected until they can begin to take care of themselves.

A southern sea otter is born in the water a few hundred yards off the coast of California. It is a sea creature — but at first it can't swim at all. All it can do is float. So the little pup spends most of its time riding around on top of its mother's furry chest as she floats on her back.

But sometimes a mother has to leave her baby to go off and feed herself. This could be a very dangerous time for the young otter. What if it drifted out to sea? What if a big wave swept it up onto the rocky shore?

But the mother sea otter makes sure this doesn't happen. Sea otters live near beds of giant seaweed called kelp. Long stringy leaves of the greenish-brown plant spread out across the top of the water.

Whenever a mother wants to leave, she picks up her baby and puts it on some of these leaves of kelp. Then she rolls the baby over and over like a ball. The strings are wrapped around the little otter's body. Now the baby can't go anywhere, even if it wants to. Soon the little otter falls fast asleep — safe in its cradle of kelp.

Even timid animals can be very brave when they are defending their young. Often they will fight when it seems they can't possibly win.

Someone once saw a rabbit kick and kick at a weasel with her hind legs until she sent it tumbling down a hill.

A shrew is one of the very smallest mammals in the world. A full-grown shrew can sit in a tablespoon — with plenty of room to spare. Yet, once a mother shrew was seen attacking a big raccoon. She won, too.

Most mammal mothers keep their babies safe all by themselves. Their mates have long since wandered away. But some mammal fathers stay with their growing families. Wolf fathers do. So do coyotes and foxes.

A father fox spends some time every day hunting for food for his mate. The rest of the time he stays near the family den. He is guarding the mother and her cubs.

When some hungry animal comes too close, the father fox may fight — if the enemy is small enough. But if a big animal like a bear gets too near, the fox protects his family another way. He runs away.

A fox can run very silently. But now the father fox makes a lot of noise. Almost always the hungry bear chases after it.

The fox runs fast, but not too fast. He doesn't want to lose that bear! And every mile or so he changes the direction he is running a little. Finally he is many miles from home. The bear will never find his family now. Suddenly the tricky fox runs much faster, and leaves the bear behind. Soon he will find his way back to the den — to guard his family again.

Many babies need to be protected at first. But scientists who study animals say the most helpless babies of all are born to animals like the kangaroo. The kangaroo mother has a pouch attached to the middle of her abdomen. It is open at the top — just like a big pocket.

A kangaroo grows inside its mother's body as all mammal babies do. But it only stays there for five weeks. Then it is born — far too soon to live in the outside world.

The newborn kangaroo is only as big as a baked bean. It has no eyes, just blue smudges where eyes will be one day. Its hind legs are two small bumps. And its skin is so thin that you might kill it if you picked it up. There is no way *this* helpless animal can take care of itself.

For a few minutes the baby rests. Then it begins to move. With its tiny front legs and claws, it climbs up its mother's rough fur. It is heading for her pouch. The trip will take three minutes — the three most dangerous minutes of the kangaroo's entire life.

A mother kangaroo can't pick anything up with her front paws. So if the baby falls it will surely die. Slowly it drags itself upward. First the left paw reaches out...and then the right...and then the left again.... Finally the tiny kangaroo gets to the top of the pouch and slips inside. Now it snuggles down into the warm fur that lines the pouch and begins to drink its mother's milk.

For the next few months, that is all that will be
seen of the baby kangaroo. Its mother hops around as
usual until one day the baby, much bigger now, pokes
its head out of the pouch.

Soon it will hop out of the pouch for the first time. A growing kangaroo spends more and more of its time out of its mother's pouch. But if it is tired or scared or hungry, it hops right back in again. In and out it pops like a jack-in-the-box. Then one day it tries to get inside the pouch as usual — and the mother kangaroo pushes it away. If it tries again she gives it a good hard punch. This probably means there is another tiny kangaroo growing in the pouch.

Sometimes an animal's mother dies. When a mother dolphin dies, the young dolphin has a pretty good chance of growing up. Often another female will feed it. And the other dolphins will keep it safe.

Any lion mother will care for another lioness's cubs. So will elephants and many members of the monkey family. But there are some animals who cannot live without their mothers.

A sheep cares only for her own lamb. If another hungry lamb tries to nurse, the mother sheep will butt and kick it away.

A fur seal mother nurses her pup for a few hours. Then she swims out to sea to feed herself. For the next three or four months she will do this again and again. Each time she comes back, she must find her own pup.

This isn't easy. Thousands of youngsters crowd together in each seal nursery. But as the mother seal comes out of the water, she begins to call to her baby. It is like a special song she has sung to her little seal since it was born.

When the seal hears the song, it begins to waddle toward the sound. Slowly the mother and child come closer and closer.

But other seal children follow the sound too. Before long the mother has a big bunch of hungry seals crowding close around her.

They are all the same size and color and shape. How can she tell them apart? She sniffs each one. She sniffs again. Then she stops. She has found her pup. She knows its own special smell.

Now she honks and hisses and snaps and snarls until all the other young seals back away. Then she lets her baby nurse.

Danger!

At first, mammal children hardly leave their mothers at all. A chimpanzee clings to its mother's body for many months. A baby whale looks like a small shadow as it glides close to its mother's side. But as animal children grow, they become more and more restless. They want to taste and touch and smell everything around them.

This can lead to exciting adventures. It can lead to trouble too. An animal's world is filled with many dangers. And it takes time to learn to be careful. So most mothers watch their young children very carefully.

Often mothers have noises or signals that mean "Watch out!" or "Don't move!"

When a mother beaver sees or hears something she doesn't like, she slaps her broad tail on the water as hard as she can. This is a beaver's way of saying something is wrong. When her little kits hear this loud slapping sound, they all dive deep in the water.

A bear's "Woof!" of warning usually brings her cubs tumbling back to her side.

A young baboon wanders and plays with other young baboons. But its mother never lets it wander far. When it does, the mother makes a soft grunting sound. "Come back," this sound means. And most of the time the baboon obeys. Sometimes it is too busy having fun to mind its mother. Then she reaches out and pulls it back by its tail.

Many young animals are cared for by their mothers alone. Some are watched over by their fathers too. Others are raised in bigger groups. Then the job of keeping them safe belongs to everyone.

Dolphins live in groups called schools. A dolphin almost never swims alone. But sometimes a young dolphin sees something interesting in the water — a strange fish, perhaps — and swims off after it.

The dolphin may swim along for a while. Then suddenly it is not alone anymore. Three sharks are circling around it, ready to attack!

The young dolphin can't possibly win such a fight. So it begins to whistle. This very sharp, very loud whistle is the dolphin's way of shouting "Help!"

The other dolphins in the school stop as soon as they hear this special whistle. Then they all speed off to rescue their young friend.

The dolphins spread out in a big circle around the sharks. They ram the sharks with their snouts. They slam them with their long, hard tails. The sharks fight back as hard as they can. But there are too many dolphins. Before long, three dead sharks sink to the bottom of the sea.

But the young dolphin has been bitten in many places. Now it is too weak to swim to the surface by itself. Quickly, two big dolphins swim beside it. Each sticks a flipper under the little dolphin's belly — and lifts it up for a breath of air. Then they sink down into the water again.

They go up and down for half an hour or so. Then two more dolphins take over the job. For the next few hours one team of dolphins after another keeps the young dolphin alive. Finally it is able to swim and breathe by itself. Then the dolphins leap into the air and swim away together.

Lessons to learn

Some animals, such as bugs and spiders and snails, are born knowing all they will ever know.

Mammals, too, are born knowing some things by *instinct*. All mammal babies just naturally cuddle close to each other and to their mothers for warmth. All babies know how to nurse.

Most mammals also grow into doing certain things as they get older. But they learn faster if they are not alone.

For the first few months a baby elephant hardly uses its trunk at all. Its muscles are too weak. But an elephant's trunk is a very important part of its body. An elephant eats and drinks with its trunk. It smells with it too.

Elephants can't see very well. But their sense of smell is so good they can tell exactly what is going on around them. When a mother elephant is angry, she may spank her baby with her trunk. And elephants that are friends often walk trunk in trunk.

A baby elephant can't do most of these things at first. But soon its trunk muscles grow stronger. It watches the big elephants, and little by little it learns to use its trunk too.

Many animals can do some things, but they don't know they can. A river otter is born on land. It can swim by the time it is three months old. But it doesn't know that. So a mother river otter tricks her young kits into taking the first swim.

Every young river otter loves to ride on its mother's back. The mother takes a little otter for long rides along the bank of a river or lake. Then one day, without any warning at all, she slides into the water and begins to swim.

The poor little otter clings to her back and wails with terror. The mother pays no attention. She paddles around for a few minutes and then climbs back onto the land again.

The young otter doesn't mind so much the next time its mother carries it into the water. After all, it is still safe and dry on top of her furry back. Then one day the mother otter swims out to the middle of the river and sinks down into the water.

At first the little otter thrashes and splashes as hard as it can. But then it stops struggling. It isn't sinking after all. It's swimming! From now on the otter will feel at home in its watery world.

So some animals are born knowing how to do certain things. And some begin to do things naturally as they grow older. But some animals must also be taught.

Most of the time they learn these lessons from their parents.

Animals that eat meat must learn to hunt. A three-month-old lion is far too young to catch another animal — even a very small, very slow one. But that's when hunting lessons begin.

A lion cub's first *prey* is its mother's tail. She lies on the ground and swishes her tail slowly from side to side. As she does this, the tip of her tail wriggles.

Again and again her cubs will crouch and pounce. Sometimes they manage to catch her tail and pin it to the ground. More often they miss. But little by little the young lions become more skillful. Before long they pounce on butterflies and small bugs. They catch a few too.

Now it is time for harder lessons. A mother lion begins to take her cubs along on real hunting trips. Perhaps she is hunting an antelope. The cubs stay behind her and try to do everything she does.

She creeps closer and closer to the antelope. The cubs creep closer too. When she crouches, they crouch. When she flattens herself and crawls along the ground, they do the same thing. When she stops and lies very still, they stop too.

One of the most important lessons any hunting animal must learn is to be patient. Often a half-grown cub doesn't move quietly enough. Or it gets bored holding still and moves a little. Then the antelope races away. But that's all right. There will be another lesson tomorrow.

Coyotes live in many parts of North America. They are at home in prairies, deserts, open woodlands, and rocky hillsides. Some people say they are the smartest hunters in the animal world. But young coyotes must also learn to be good hunters.

A rabbit makes a very tasty meal for a coyote. But rabbits can run much faster than coyotes can. So the mother and father coyote teach their pups to hunt in pairs. The coyote youngsters sit very still and watch their parents' every move.

Rabbits, like many animals, run in large circles when they are being chased. So the mother coyote starts after the rabbit. The father coyote takes a shortcut across to the other side of the circle. He

hides behind a bush or a rock until the rabbit comes
zipping by. Then he takes up the chase while the
mother rests for a while.

The mother and father coyote keep taking turns
until the rabbit is too tired to run anymore. Then the

whole family settles down to share a meal. Before long the young coyotes will be working in teams too.

Hunting animals must also learn what *not* to eat. At first a bear will tear into any animal it can catch. But it soon learns to be more careful. A shrew might look like a tasty mouse. But it tastes very bitter.

And all its life a bear never forgets what an angry skunk smells like.

A young fox gets a face full of quills only once. Then it learns to leave a porcupine alone.

Animals who are hunted by other animals have important lessons to learn too. Lesson number one is: *Be alert! Watch out for danger at all times!*

Lesson number two is just as important: *Know who your enemies are.*

Most babies aren't born knowing who will harm them and who won't. Their mothers must show them which animals to fear.

A mother chimpanzee with her baby will share the same water hole with many animals — even very big ones like elephants. But if a hungry leopard comes too close, the mother chimp grows very tense. Then, with

her baby clinging tight, she runs away. Soon the young chimpanzee learns to fear these dangerous animals too.

All animals grow up to take care of themselves. But animals who live their whole lives in groups must learn another kind of lesson. They must learn how to live with each other.

Most animals let babies do whatever they want. Very young animals haven't had enough time to learn how to behave. But as animal children grow they must learn to mind their manners — or they will soon be sorry.

Often a young animal plays too roughly. Or makes too much noise. Or wakes someone up. Then some adult warns it to stop.

An angry lioness twitches her tail very fast.

A bear growls deep in her throat.

A mother dolphin warns her children by opening and closing her mouth. This makes a loud, clapping sound.

An old male baboon simply raises his eyebrows and stares hard at the young baboon who is bothering him. Or he may thump his hairy fist on the ground.

Usually this is enough to make a young animal stop what it is doing. But sometimes a youngster is having too much fun to stop. Then it is punished.

A lioness will roll her cub over on its back and hold it down with her paw.

A bear will spank her child, but she is careful not to hurt it with her long, sharp claws.

A mother dolphin pushes her young one down in the water and simply holds it down for a minute or so.

An angry baboon chases a naughty child and nips it on the shoulder. The bite doesn't really hurt. But it will make the young baboon finally pay some attention!

Quickly the little baboon crouches and peers over its shoulder at the bigger baboon. If the old male is still angry, the young baboon grins widely and smacks its lips together. This is a baboon's way of saying, "I'm sorry." The apology is always accepted. These big monkeys, like most wild animals, never stay angry for long.

Animals learn what they must know in many ways. Sometimes they learn by watching what other animals do, and then trying to do the same things too. Sometimes they are tricked into learning. Sometimes they are taught. And sometimes they must learn by being put in their place now and then.

Animals also learn in another, much more pleasant way — by playing.

At first babies play alone. A human baby plays with its fingers and toes. Very young animals chew and suck on their paws. They roll around on the ground. They run in circles chasing their tails.

As animals grow older they begin to spend more and more time playing with friends.

Mountain goats usually live in high, rocky places. So young goats grow more and more sure-footed as they play follow-the-leader, leaping from rock to rock.

Animals that hunt often play pouncing games.

And animals that must move very fast to escape danger spend a lot of time racing after one another.

Animal children often play the same games that human children do. Young squirrel monkeys play tug-of-war with vines. Tag is a favorite dolphin game. Bears wrestle or play hide-and-seek. River otters love to slide.

All this rough-and-tumble play helps a growing animal become stronger and more skillful. Does playing help a young animal grow in still another way?

Two scientists named Harry and Margaret Harlow decided to find out. They wanted to know if playing together helps young animals like monkeys and apes grow into happy adults.

They took some baby macaque monkeys and divided them into three groups. Each monkey was put in a separate cage.

The babies in Group One never got to see or play with other young monkeys.

The monkeys in Group Two didn't get to play with each other, either. But they could see other young monkeys sitting in their cages across the room.

The monkeys in Group Three were allowed to romp and roll with each other for 20 minutes a day. Then they were put back in their separate cages once more.

What happened to these different monkeys as they grew up?

The monkeys in Group One just sat in their cages, doing nothing. When they were put in a room with other monkeys, they were terribly frightened. All their lives these monkeys would never be able to make friends.

The story of the monkeys in Group Two is sad too. As soon as any two monkeys got close to one another they began to fight. There was no way these monkeys would ever be friends either.

And the monkeys in the third group? Their story had a much happier ending. At first they were a little shy with each other when they were put in the same room. But before long they were sharing all sorts of monkey games.

Twenty minutes of play a day isn't much. But it was enough to help these animals get along with each other for the rest of their lives.

Time to begin life on their own

Some animals have a very short childhood. A rabbit hops away to begin life alone in just four weeks. A female field mouse becomes a mother herself when she is only six weeks old. Other animal childhoods last much longer. But finally, for all, the moment comes — the time to say good-bye.

Of course some animals stay near their family groups even after they are grown. Dolphins do. So do whales and chimpanzees. A female elephant and her mother often remain best friends for life. And many wolves stay in the same pack year after year.

But for most, a time comes to begin living on their own. One of the first things a mother black bear teaches her two cubs is to climb a tree. A bear child soon learns that it must stay up in that tree until its mother tells it to come down.

One day the mother sends her almost-grown children up some tall tree as usual. But this time she doesn't tell them to come down. She will be miles away before they grow hungry enough to disobey. Very likely they will never see their mother again. From now on they will take care of themselves.

But most animals don't find saying good-bye hard at all. One day they just wander off by themselves — and don't come back.

Before long they will find a mate, and the story of family life will begin again as they feed, and care for, and teach young ones of their own.

INDEX

Page numbers in brown mean there is only a little bit of information about the animal on that page. Page numbers in black mean there is more complete information.